SONATINA ALBUM

A Collection of Favorite Sonatinas, Rondos and Other Pieces

COMPILED BY LOUIS KÖHLER • EDITED BY ALLAN SMALL

This newly edited edition eliminates impractical fingerings, awkward page turns and unnecessary accidentals. The newly engraved music creates cleaner-looking pages that are easier and more enjoyable to read.

CONTENTS

A cassette (#4053) or CD (#3997) recording of the selections contained in *Sonatina Album*, beautifully performed by Kim O'Reilly, is available separately.

Second Edition
Copyright © MCMXCII by Alfred Publishing Co., Inc.
All rights reseved. Printed in USA

Cover art: Still Life with Lemons, Oranges and a Rose
by Francisco de Zurbarán (Spanish, 1598–1664).
Oil on canvas, 1633.
The Norton Simon Foundation, Pasadena, California

LAY-FLAT BINDING

Alfred has made every effort to make this book not only attractive, but more convenient and long-lasting as well. Most books larger than 96 pages do not lie flat or stay open easily. In addition, the pages in these books (which are usually glued together) tend to break away from the spine after repeated use.

In Alfred's special lay-flat binding editions for large books, pages are sewn together in multiples of 16, preventing pages from falling out of the book while still allowing it to stay open easily. Alfred also offers another type of special binding for large books called plastic comb binding. This format allows the book to lie open even flatter than the lay-flat binding.

We hope that these long-lasting, convenient bindings will encourage additional use of our publications and will continue to bring added pleasure to you for years to come.

SONATINA

(In G)

Ludwig van Beethoven

Romanze

PRELUDE
from The Well-Tempered Clavier

Johann Sebastian Bach

* This measure may be omitted. Its authenticity has not been verified.

a) suggested by the editor

SONATINA
Op. 36, No. 1

Muzio Clementi

SONATINA

Op.36, No.2

Muzio Clementi

Allegretto

* (poco rit.)

(a tempo)

* (poco rit.)

* suggested by the editor

Allegro

SONATINA

Op.36, No.3

Muzio Clementi

* In some editions this G is not tied to the previous G.

a)

Un poco Adagio

SONATINA

Op.36, No.4

Muzio Clementi

Con spirito

* The editor suggests a *fortissimo* entrance like the beginning of the sonata.

20

Andante con espressione

Rondo
Allegro vivace

Da Capo
al Fine

SONATINA
Op.36, No.5

Muzio Clementi

25

AIR SUISSE
Allegro moderato

* suggested by the editor

Rondo
Allegro di molto

da capo al Fine

SONATINA
Op.36, No.6

Allegro con spirito

Muzio Clementi

36

Rondo
Allegretto spiritoso

SONATINA

Op.151, No.1

Antonio Diabelli

Scherzo
Allegro

Rondo
Allegretto

43

SONATINA
Op. 20, No. 1

Jan Ladislav Dussek

Allegro non tanto

Rondo
Allegretto Tempo di Minuetto

Major

SONATINA
Op. 20, No. 1

Friedrich Kuhlau

Andante

Rondo
Allegro

SONATINA

Op. 20, No. 2

Friedrich Kuhlau

Adagio e sostenuto

Allegro scherzando

SONATINA
Op. 20, No. 3

Friedrich Kuhlau

Allegro con spirito

con espressione e sostenuto assai

68

Larghetto
sostenuto

70

Alla Polacca

SONATINA

Op.55, No.1

Friedrich Kuhlau

SONATINA
Op.55, No.2

Friedrich Kuhlau

Allegretto

SONATINA
Op. 55, No. 3

Friedrich Kuhlau

Allegro con spirito

Allegretto grazioso

SONATA

Franz Joseph Haydn

Adagio

Finale
Allegro

* *(poco rit.)* is suggested by the editor.
a) The fermata may be observed by adding an extra measure at this point.

a) see similar letter on previous page.

SONATA
(K.545)

Wolfgang Amadeus Mozart

Rondo
Allegretto

SONATA

Op. 49, No. 2

Ludwig van Beethoven

Allegro, ma non troppo

a)

Tempo di Minuetto

SONATA
Op. 49, No. 1

Ludwig van Beethoven

118

Rondo
Allegro

RONDO

Wolfgang Amadeus Mozart

RONDO

Op. 51, No.1

Ludwig van Beethoven

Moderato e grazioso

134

ANDANTE
from the "SURPRISE" SYMPHONY

Franz Joseph Haydn

IMPROMPTU
"ROSAMUNDE"

Franz   Schubert

ANDANTE GRAZIOSO

Franz Joseph Haydn

ADAGIO

Franz Joseph Haydn

ANDANTE
from the FIRST SYMPHONY

Ludwig van Beethoven

Andante cantabile con moto